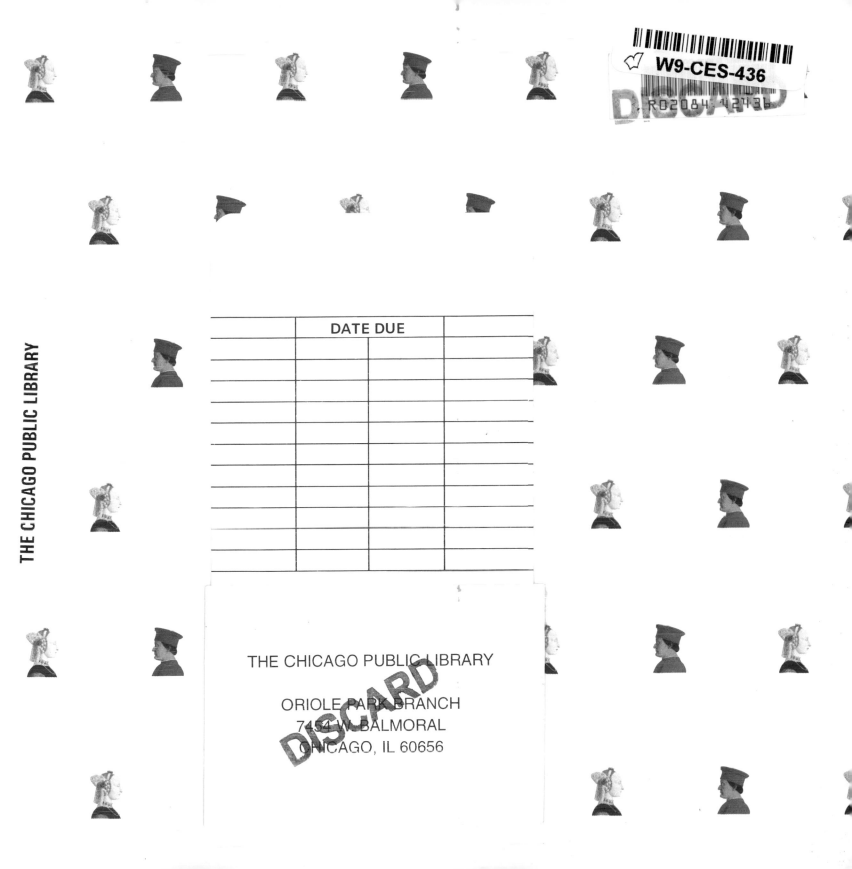

The
ART
GALLERY

FACES

The
ART
GALLERY

FACES

Written by

Philip Wilkinson

Series editor

Alison Cole

PETER BEDRICK BOOKS

NTC/Contemporary Publishing Group

NEW YORK

ACKNOWLEDGMENTS

a = above, **b** = below, **l** = left, **r** = right

6 Louvre, Paris/Bridgeman Art Library, **8** Georgia Lee, courtesy Paul Bahn, **9l & r** Ancient Art & Architecture Collection, **10l** British Museum, London, **10r** Ancient Art & Architecture Collection, **11 l** San Vitale, Ravenna/Scala, **11r** Private Collection, Athens/AKG, **12l** Uffizi, Florence/Scala, **12r** Alte Pinakothek, Munich/AKG, **13l** Gemäldegalerie, Dresden/Bridgeman Art Library, **13r** National Gallery, London, **14l** Louvre, Paris/AKG/Erich Lessing, **14r** The Royal Collection © 1997 Her Majesty Queen Elizabeth II, **15l & r & 16l** National Gallery, London, **16r** © The Iveagh Bequest, Kenwood/English Heritage, **17l** © The Frick Collection, New York, **17r** Abby Aldrich Rockefeller Folk Art Center, Williamsburg, VA, **18l** National Gallery of Art, Washington, Chester Dale Collection, **18r** Oesterreichisches Gallerie im Belvedere/AKG/Erich Lessing, **19l** Tate Gallery, London, **19r** Scottish National Gallery of Modern Art, Edinburgh, **20 & 21l** Uffizi, Florence/Scala, **22** Louvre, Paris/ Bridgeman Art Library, **23l** The Royal Collection © 1997 Her Majesty Queen Elizabeth II, **23c** National Gallery of Art, Washington/ Bridgeman Art Library, **23r** Biblioteca Reale, Torino/AKG, **24** National Gallery, London/ Bridgeman Art Library, **25l** Galleria Nazionale d'Arte Antica, Rome/Scala, **25c** The Royal Collection © 1997 Her Majesty Queen Elizabeth II, **25r** Uffizi, Florence/AKG, **26** Metropolitan Museum of Art, New York/Bridgeman Art Library, **27l** Prado, Madrid/AKG, **27b** Galleria Doria Pamphili, Rome/Scala, **28** National Gallery, London, **29l & r** Mauritshuis, The Hague/Bridgeman Art Library, **29b** Kupferstichkabinett Staatliche Museen zu Berlin-Preussischer Kulturbesitz, **30** Mauritshuis, The Hague, inv. no. 670, **31l** Louvre, Paris/AKG/Erich Lessing, **31b** The Royal Collection © 1997 Her Majesty Queen Elizabeth II, **31r** Mauritshuis, The Hague/Giraudon/ Bridgeman Art Library, **32** © Sterling & Francine Clark Art Institute, Williamstown, Massachusetts, USA, **33a** Courtauld Institute Gallery, London/Bridgeman Art Library, **33b** Phillips Collection, Washington/Bridgeman Art Library, **33r** Galerie Daniel Malingue, Paris/Bridgeman Art Library, **34** Musée d'Orsay, Paris/Giraudon/ Bridgeman Art Library, **35l** Private Collection/Bridgeman Art Library, **35b** National Gallery, London **35r** Courtauld Institute Gallery, London/Bridgeman Art Library, **36** Tate Gallery, London © Succession Picasso/DACS 1997, **37l** Pushkin Museum, Moscow/Bridgeman Art Library © Succession Picasso /DACS 1997, **37b** Art Institute of Chicago, Gift of Mrs Gilbert W. Chapman, 1948.561, Pablo Picasso, Spanish 1881-1973, Daniel-Henry Kahnweiler, oil on canvas, 1910, 100.6 x 72.8cm, photograph © 1993 The Art Institute of Chicago, All Rights Reserved, **37r** Henri Cartier Bresson/Magnum Photos, **38** Musée National d'Art Moderne, Paris, **39l** San Francisco Museum of Modern Art, Albert M. Bender Collection, Gift of Albert M. Bender, **39b & r** © Gisèle Freund/John Hilleson Agency, **40b** Alte Pinakothek, Munich/AKG, **40r** Palazzo Ducale, Mantua/Scala, **41a & r** National Portrait Gallery, London, **42l** The Royal Collection ©1997 Her Majesty Queen Elizabeth II, **42r** Musée Carnavalet, Paris/Giraudon, **43l** National Gallery, London **43r** © Macmillan Children's Books **44l** Victoria & Albert Museum, London, **44r & 45l** British Museum, London, **45r, 46l & r** Victoria & Albert Museum, London, **46b** British Museum, London, **47a** Victoria & Albert Museum, London, **47r** British Library, London/Bridgeman Art Library.

CONTENTS

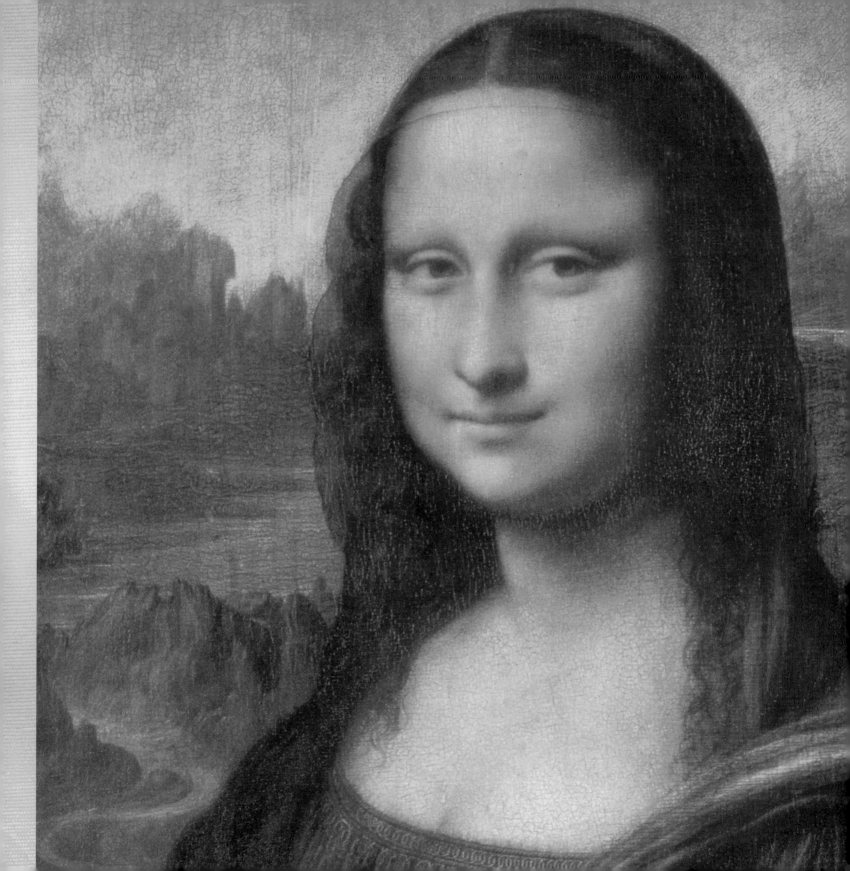

INTRODUCTION

Faces are fascinating. Every single human face is different, and our faces change over the years as we grow older, and from moment to moment when we are in different moods.

Portraits have been painted for thousands of years, and artists have used their great skills in painting, drawing, and sculpting faces. In ancient times, the most common faces to be portrayed were those of gods and kings. Later, it became fashionable for rich people to have their portraits painted. They often wanted paintings that made them look attractive, but some artists were unwilling simply to flatter their subjects (the people they painted). The artists also wanted to show their subjects' real character as well as their outward appearance. Today, nearly everyone collects portraits of themselves and their friends—although they are almost always photographs rather than paintings.

This book shows some of the great variety of portraits through the ages. It is divided into three sections. The first is a historical section, showing how portraits have developed from early images of the gods to the work of modern painters. The second part presents a selection of ten of the world's greatest portraits, together with information about other works by these artists. Finally, the third section looks at proportions and caricature, and the variety of art around the world. The three sections of the book make up an exciting collection of images of people, both world-famous and little-known, and of different artists' ways of showing the appearance and character of the people they painted.

ANCIENT AND MEDIEVAL

The earliest artists were those of the ancient world. They produced images of their kings which showed royal power, and pictures of their gods which could be worshiped. In each case the face in the picture symbolized, or stood for, the very idea of royalty or holiness. These images were stylized (created using a particular style which does not show things as they are in real life).

In images of symbolic faces the most important aspect is showing the idea that the face represents, rather than a likeness of one particular person. Artists included clues to show a person's status. For example, in ancient Egypt, only the king could wear the ceremonial beard and striped head cloth. Today we still recognize symbols like these. A person wearing a crown is a king or queen; someone with a halo above their head is a holy Christian figure.

EASTER ISLAND STATUE
The people of this Pacific island, Easter Island, erected huge stone statues, like this one, in groups around the coast. No one knows exactly how old the statues are or how they were made, but they were probably carved at least 1,000 years ago. The statues would have been very difficult to put up without complex machinery. The highest statue is 33 feet high!

All the figures have similar features, including long noses and ears, and strange flat-topped heads. The statues probably symbolize the chiefs of the island who had died and become gods after death.

FUNERARY MASK OF TUTANKHAMUN
1329 BC

This magnificent mask was placed over the mummy of the Egyptian pharaoh, Tutankhamun, when his body was buried in 1329 BC. It is made of gold, glass, and lapis lazuli, a precious blue stone, and these expensive materials show how rich the kings of Egypt were.

The young king's face is surrounded by symbols of his kingship. As well as the striped head cloth and the ceremonial beard, the artist has included a vulture and a cobra on the king's forehead. These were the symbols of the twin kingdoms of Upper and Lower Egypt which he ruled.

ANCIENT GREEK MASK
16th century BC

This mask is made of pure, beaten gold. It was the funerary mask of one of the great kings from the city of Mycenae, the capital of an ancient empire in southern Greece. It was found in the grave circle, just outside the city walls, and would have covered the face of the ruler when he was buried. The archaeologist who dug it up thought that it had been made for King Agamemnon, the famous ruler who led the Greeks at the siege of Troy. But the mask was not made to look like Agamemnon or any other king. The face was shaped to show a stylized "kingly" face which symbolized the idea of kingship, rather than to show the face of one king in particular.

Portraits from the ancient Greek and Roman empires often look very naturalistic (as the people would look in real life). Artists learned how to show the structure of the human face more accurately. Sculptures of the Roman emperors, for example, were usually carved with great skill by the finest artists of the empire. They became important symbols of the power of the emperors.

During the Middle Ages the Christian church became very powerful. Painters tried to imagine the faces of Jesus, Mary and the saints. They painted them and filled the churches with their images. These showed the greatness of the church and helped people worship. At this time it was much less important to produce the naturalistic images which were to become so popular again during the Renaissance.

BRONZE HEAD OF AUGUSTUS

1st century BC

Roman Emperors had statues of themselves put up all over the empire. This was to remind people that the Romans ruled their lands. Augustus, the first emperor, had a bronze statue put up in Upper Egypt. When local tribesmen from Meroe raided Upper Egypt, they broke the head off the statue and took it away with them. They then buried it under the steps leading to their temple of Victory. Anyone entering the temple would then be insulting the emperor by stepping on his head!

ROMANO-EGYPTIAN WAX PORTRAIT

2nd century AD

For thousands of years the Egyptians mummified their dead and buried them in coffins which were decorated with a picture of the person who had died. During the Roman period, when Egypt was ruled by the Romans, these pictures became more naturalistic. They were often painted onto a smooth wooden panel and are very different from the stylized funerary masks used in the time of Tutankhamun (page 9).

MOSAIC OF THE EMPEROR JUSTINIAN AND HIS SERVANTS (*detail*) *6th century AD*

The Byzantines ruled a large empire based in the city of Constantinople (now Istanbul, Turkey) and including the eastern half of the ancient Roman empire. Their artists produced glittering mosaics using small pieces of colored stones, glass, and gold leaf. The church of San Vitale, Ravenna, contains a stunning mosaic which includes this detail of the emperor Justinian, who was one of their powerful emperors and ruled from AD 527 to 565. Justinian's jeweled crown and the ornate brooch on his cloak show that he is an emperor, while the halo around his head is a sign of his Christian faith.

THE AWAKENING OF LAZARUS
A Christian Icon, 12th century

Icons are small pictures of Jesus, the Virgin Mary, or a saint, painted on wooden panels. They are used during prayer and may also be carried in religious processions. The subject of an icon can usually be recognized by certain features. In this painting, for example, Jesus is shown with the traditional symbols of halo and cross.

The word "icon" itself comes from the Greek word for "likeness:" by creating a "likeness" the artist helped people feel closer to the saint or holy person they worshiped. This icon tells the story of a miracle. Jesus is waking Lazarus from the dead.

Renaissance

During the fifteenth century western art changed dramatically. Artists looked back to the art of ancient Greece and Rome for inspiration. They also began to look more closely at the real world, and especially at the features of real people. This change led to the artistic movement called the Renaissance (the name comes from the French for "rebirth") which spread through Italy and Northern Europe. Artists continued to paint religious subjects but now they based their saints on actual people whom they used as models. Rich people also wanted to have their portraits painted so that their faces and actions would then be remembered long after they were dead. Many dukes and princes became the patrons, or employers, of artists, and the names of artists became important as they became famous as individuals.

THE BIRTH OF VENUS (*detail*)
Sandro Botticelli, 1445–1510
During the Renaissance, people thought of Venus, the Roman goddess of love, as an image of ideal beauty which would inspire people to noble thoughts and actions. For his picture of Venus, from which this detail is taken, Botticelli created the most beautiful face he could think of—with pale skin like marble, flowing hair, and radiant eyes. The artist used fine lines of real gold in the hair to make it shimmer as it blows in the wind.

SELF-PORTRAIT *Albrecht Dürer, 1471–1528*
In this self-portrait the German artist, Dürer, gave himself the beard and shoulder-length hair which were always used to show the image of Jesus Christ. By painting himself as Christ, Dürer was showing that the powers of the artist are "god-given." This idea reflects the fact that artists were becoming more and more respected as creative and highly-trained people.

MAN WITH A BLUE SLEEVE
Titian, c. 1480–1576

During Titian's long life, he became a very famous Italian painter—but it was his skill as a portrait painter which was most admired. Titian liked to paint without making any rough drawings first. In this painting he has used the oil paint to show the shimmering fabric of the sleeve and the fine details of the man's face.

Titian's man is leaning over the window sill, looking out of the painting at the viewer. He looks as if he has just turned around and caught the viewer's eye. This was an original way of painting a portrait at the time, as it does not show the sitter in a formal pose.

THE SISTINE MADONNA (*detail*)
Raphael, 1483–1520

This is a detail of Italian artist Raphael's *Sistine Madonna* which was painted for the monks of the church of St. Sisto in a town called Piacenza. For this image of the Madonna (the Virgin Mary) he used Margherita Luti as a model. She was the daughter of a baker in Rome, who was much admired by the young men of her district—including Raphael himself. It is said that the artist often used to break off from his work to go and see Margherita, so it is not surprising that he should have included her in a painting. Her gentle beauty is caught by Raphael's soft brushstrokes which also give the painting a feeling of perfect stillness and calm.

16TH AND 17TH CENTURIES

During the sixteenth and seventeenth centuries, artists tried to introduce more drama into their paintings. Many portraits show more contrast between the light and dark areas in the picture, so that faces seem to glow in the shadows or emerge from a mysterious or gloomy background. Artists explored the variety of light and color and became more adventurous with the sort of poses they used, painting their subjects from different angles.

AUTUMN *Giuseppe Arcimboldo, 1527–1593*
Arcimboldo developed a way of painting fantastic heads, made out of collections of smaller objects. A head could be made up of books, animals, flowers, or, as here, fruit and plants. Arcimboldo worked for the Hapsburg emperors, who lived in Prague and ruled much of central Europe. This painting was done as a tribute to the emperor Rudolf II, who was a keen gardener.

SELF-PORTRAIT AS THE ART OF PAINTING
Artemisia Gentileschi, 1593–1652
The artist shows herself concentrating carefully on her painting. The way in which we view her face from the side adds to the interest of the picture. The dramatic lighting focuses our attention on the artist's face, arm, and neck, as they emerge brilliantly out of the shadows.

PEASANT BOY LEANING ON A SILL

Bartolomé Estebán Murillo, 1617–82

Murillo was a very successful painter and, as well as many religious paintings, he often painted portraits of peasants and beggars on the streets of his native Seville, in Spain. In this painting, Murillo shows a peasant boy who, despite being dressed in ragged clothes, has been given a cheerful smile by the artist. Murillo has given the painting a warm and gentle light which adds to the feeling of contentment.

Portraits like this proved very popular in seventeenth century Spain. Rich people liked to buy these paintings of poor children as they thought it showed that the poor could be happy.

YOUNG MAN HOLDING A SKULL

Frans Hals, c. 1581–1666

The Dutch painter Frans Hals was famous for his portraits. He worked very quickly, often showing people at a particular moment in time: smiling, drinking, laughing, talking, and pointing. In this portrait he brushed on a reddish-brown background, then painted directly on top of it. Some of the facial features are sketched in with a few hasty brushstrokes, giving the portrait a lively quality.

The skull is a reminder that, although the sitter is young and healthy, there must come a time when, like everyone else, he will die.

18th and Early 19th Centuries

The eighteenth century saw a huge increase in the demand for portraits. Artists like Perronneau traveled around painting and drawing the rich families of Europe. Many artists also portrayed members of the European aristocracy. People often wanted to be painted with their possessions as a symbol of their wealth, and artists were asked to include grand houses, lands, jewelery, and animals. It was an age of glamorous clothes, of rich velvets and satins. Artists learned to devote as much skill to reproducing these shimmering fabrics as they did to painting the faces of the people who sat for them.

GIRL WITH A KITTEN
Jean-Baptiste Perronneau, 1715–1783
Perronneau had few rivals as a portrait painter in France. His work was popular among the middle classes for its charm and its bright colors. His *Girl with a Kitten* is drawn in pastels, which give the picture a melting softness. She is dressed, in the fashion of the time, as if she were an adult, and her pose is very formal. Her kitten is as carefully drawn as its owner.

THE LAUGHING GIRL
Joshua Reynolds, 1723–1792
In this portrait, the artist has captured a casual, more naturalistic pose. All the light in the painting is thrown on the girl's head, arms, and dress. The fabric is painted in thick strokes, which follow the folds in the cloth, but the skin is painted with smoother brushwork. The shadows across her mouth and eyes make the viewer look closer to see whether she is really laughing, or whether her mouth is curved in a gentle smile.

THE COMTESSE D'HAUSSONVILLE

Jean-Auguste-Dominique Ingres, 1780–1867

In this picture, Ingres shows his great skill in painting details—especially the features of the Comtesse's face and the folds of her dress. Ingres was fascinated by the art of ancient Greece and Rome. He portrayed faces with all the smoothness of an ancient Greek marble statue. The artist has included the details of her home surroundings, and her clear reflection can be seen in the mirror behind. Ingres was popular with ladies in French society because he made them look so perfect and elegant.

BOY HOLDING DOG

Noah North, 1809–1880

Noah North belongs to the American group of naive painters. Their paintings have a fresh, childlike approach, which is simple, still and flat. North made a living painting signs, carriages, people's houses, and portraits in various towns in New York state. This portrait is typical of his work. The white face stands out against a dark background, but the portrait itself has little depth. The dog is also painted flat—almost as if it were a cardboard cut-out.

North's work was popular in his neighborhood, but he seems to have painted few portraits towards the end of his life. As the camera was invented around this time, his clients probably began to have photographs taken of themselves instead of sitting for portraits.

IMPRESSIONISM TO MODERN ART

 Towards the end of the nineteenth century, many artists decided to break away from traditional styles and to paint in new ways. In France, the Impressionists developed methods of showing the different effects of light on their subjects, using loose brushstrokes. Many other new styles emerged later, from the very decorative art in Vienna to the angular style of Cubism (see Picasso, page 37). Today, photography can be used to give an exact likeness of a person. Painters have explored many different ways to capture a person's appearance and character, and have used portraiture to experiment with the color and quality of paint.

TWO YOUNG LADIES IN A LOGE
Mary Cassatt, 1844–1926
American painter Mary Cassatt lived in Paris, where she painted these ladies in a "loge" ("box"), at a time when the theater was a fashionable place to go. In this painting one of the young ladies is shyly hiding behind her fan.

PORTRAIT OF ADELE BLOCH-BAUER
Gustav Klimt, 1862–1918
Gustav Klimt painted this rich portrait in 1907 in Vienna, Austria. Adele's pale face and dark hair stand out in a sea of sparkling gold decoration, covering her dress, her chair and even the surrounding walls. Klimt used a style based on mosaics in this painting and introduced extra elements into the pattern, such as the "B"s from Adele's initials.

THE LITTLE PEASANT

Amedeo Modigliani, 1884–1920

Unlike many artists, who painted rich people to earn money, Modigliani was interested in painting ordinary people, like this young man from the South of France. In his paintings and sculptures, Modigliani often stylized his sitters' faces, making their heads, noses and necks look longer than they really were, and painting them with small facial features. *The Little Peasant* looks very youthful, with his smooth face and rosy cheeks.

HEAD OF E.O.W.

Frank Auerbach, born 1931

This portrait is one of several that British artist Frank Auerbach painted of this female model. Auerbach applies the paint very quickly, producing trails, threads and waves of paint across the whole surface of the picture. This fast way of working, with a small range of colors, building up the paint at great speed, is very risky. If Auerbach does not get the result he wants, he has to scrape the paint off the canvas and start again. Sometimes it takes many efforts to get the effect the artist wants.

In this picture the paint is so thick that it stands above the canvas in thick ridges, almost like a sculpture. Auerbach has created a very modern portrait, in chaotic shades of grey, white, and black, in which the features of the face can only just be seen. The painting creates the image of an old, strong and powerful person.

PIERO DELLA FRANCESCA

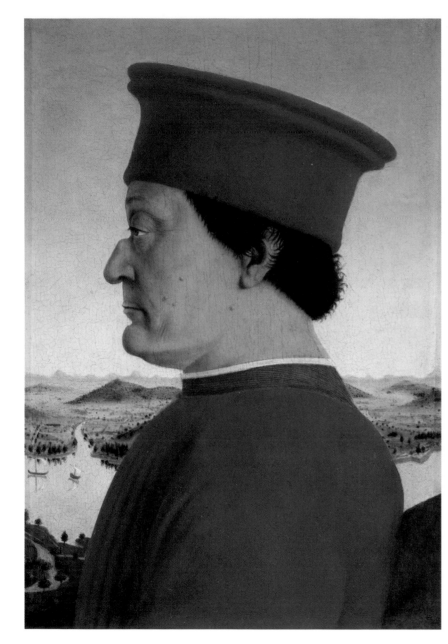

PORTRAIT OF FEDERICO DA MONTEFELTRO

Federico da Montefeltro was a famous general and count of Urbino in Italy. He was also famous as a scholar and patron of the arts. He chose Piero della Francesca to paint portraits of himself and his wife, Battista, who had recently died. The portraits were painted to celebrate one of Federico's great military victories and as a memorial to his wife.

Profile portraits, showing one side of the face, were very popular at the time as they reminded people of Roman coins, where the head of the emperor was shown in profile. Profile portraits became symbols of power and importance for men such as Federico. In his youth, Federico had suffered from a skin disease which left him scarred on the jaw. As a young man he had also lost his right eye and the bridge of his nose when he was hit by his opponent's lance in a tournament. This is why Piero chose his left-hand side, to show his undamaged eye. But Piero included his patron's scars, and his rough skin.

Piero uses the curve of the count's eyelash to suggest the original line of the nose.

PORTRAIT OF BATTISTA SFORZA

This is the companion picture to Piero's portrait of Federico da Montefeltro. His wife, Battista, is wearing the red and gold jewelery appropriate to a countess, and her dress is a dark blue. These rich colors show off her pale skin. In the fifteenth century, light skin coloring was thought to be the most beautiful for a woman. One writer of the period told artists to paint women "white" and men "brown"—exactly what Piero did in the portraits of Federico and Battista.

This figure, from one of Piero's altar-piece paintings, is thought to be a self-portrait. The same figure can also be seen in Resurrection.

Piero della Francesca was born between 1410 and 1420 in the Italian town of Sansepolcro. He spent much of his life in this town, painting pictures for local churches. He also visited Florence and Rome, and painted a famous group of frescoes in the church of San Francesco at Arezzo. In later years he worked at the court of Federico da Montefeltro, at Urbino.

Towards the end of his life Piero stopped painting. This may have been because of problems with his eyesight. Instead, he concentrated on writing two books about painting. After his death in 1492 his work was largely forgotten outside Italy, but he is now regarded as one of the greatest of Renaissance artists.

RESURRECTION

The magistrates of the Italian town of Sansepolcro asked Piero to paint this wall painting of the resurrection of Christ. The resurrection was the symbol of their town ("Sansepolcro" means "Sacred tomb"). Piero produced one of his most brilliant paintings. The solemn face of Christ has tremendous power. Piero used a feather or the tip of his finger to apply the delicately blended paint in the shadows of the painting.

LEONARDO DA VINCI

MONA LISA

A round 1503, an Italian nobleman, Francesco del Giocondo, decided to commission Leonardo da Vinci to paint a portrait of Lisa, his 24-year-old wife. The picture, now known as *Mona Lisa*, is the most famous portrait ever painted. In the painting, Leonardo's gentle use of light and shadow shape the face expertly.

Mona Lisa is famous for her smile, in which only one side of her mouth is turned upwards. Several books were published during the Renaissance period telling women how to behave gracefully. They recommended just this sort of smile. Leonardo knew that it would be difficult for his sitter to keep smiling like this while he was painting and it was said he employed a group of musicians to play and joke as he worked. Leonardo worked on this painting for three years and kept it in his studio. The King of France liked the picture so much that he bought it from Leonardo in 1516.

Leonardo used a technique called "sfumato" (from the Italian word for "smoke") to create a soft, shadowy effect around the eyes.

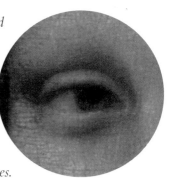

Drawing from Nature

Leonardo filled his notebooks with thousands of drawings of everything he saw around him, including castles, horses and plants. He even dissected corpses to find out about the body's bones and muscles, making drawings like these studies of the human skull. Leonardo wanted to work out the ideal proportions of the face and body, and drew lines across the skull to show the sizes of the different parts. He then used this knowledge in his paintings.

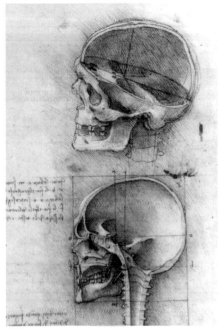

Drawing of the human skull, 1498. Leonardo often added notes in curious back-to-front writing that could only be read in a mirror.

GINEVRA DE'BENCI

This was the first portrait that Leonardo painted. It shows Ginevra de'Benci, the wife of a merchant from Florence. Ginevra's name is similar to the Italian word for "juniper" ("ginepro"), so Leonardo included a juniper bush behind her head. The clear lines and the contrasts between her pale skin and the dark background show that Leonardo had not yet developed the "sfumato" technique of *Mona Lisa*.

This powerful self-portrait was drawn by Leonardo in red chalk when he was 60.

Leonardo was born in 1452 in the town of Vinci, in Italy. As a teenager he was apprenticed to the leading artist Andrea Verrocchio in Florence, before he had his own artist's studio. He worked for Italian noble families, painting portraits and religious scenes, and designing buildings and deadly machines of war. Leonardo was also a scientist and an inventor. He designed items such as a flying machine with flapping wings, a form of helicopter, and a parachute; although none of these was ever built.

Leonardo da Vinci experimented with new ideas and often left his paintings unfinished in his rush to get on to the next project. He died in France at the age of 67.

HANS HOLBEIN

LADY WITH A SQUIRREL AND A STARLING

Holbein made his first visit to England from Germany in the 1520s, and this was probably when he painted this portrait. No one knows who the young woman in the picture was. The bird, a starling, may be a clue as to her identity—it may have appeared on her coat-of-arms.

The picture shows Holbein's genius for painting different materials. The lady's fur cap, shawl, and the upper part of her dress are all white. But the artist's fine brushwork has caught the difference between their textures.

The squirrel was probably a family pet. It was painted last, and Holbein had to change the sitter's hands and arms when he painted them holding the animal. Some experts think that he may have had to use another person's hands as the model for this part of the painting. This may be why the hands are slightly darker and less smooth than the lady's face and neck.

Holbein used tiny patches of white paint for the shining highlights on the squirrel's eye and paw. Single strokes with a fine brush pick out hairs and whiskers.

KING HENRY VIII

It is this image of Henry VIII that is one of the best known of any English king. The big body is made still more bulky by thick layers of expensive clothes, adding to an image of power and splendor. Holbein took great care with both the king's face and his clothes. The individual hairs of the beard and the wrinkles around the eyes are painted with pin-sharp accuracy. The chain, buttons, and thread are painted with real gold.

HENRY BRANDON, 2ND DUKE OF SUFFOLK

Holbein painted several portrait miniatures, including this painting of the five-year-old Duke of Suffolk. It was very fashionable to have miniature portraits of your family painted at the time. This tiny picture is only 2 inches across (the size it is shown here) and the artist painted it using watercolors. But the details, especially of the boy's hair and eyes, and the fur trim on his cap, are just as carefully painted as in Holbein's larger portraits in oils.

Holbein drew this self-portrait when he was 45. He used black and colored chalks on pink-tinted paper.

Hans Holbein was born in 1497/8. Both his father (also called Hans) and his brother Ambrosius were painters, and Hans was trained in his father's workshop in Augsburg, Germany. When he was a teenager, he went to work in Basle, in Switzerland, as a book illustrator and portrait painter. Holbein left Switzerland for England with a letter of recommendation to Sir Thomas Moore, the king's chancellor. He soon became the official Court Painter to King Henry VIII and painted portraits of the royal family and members of the English nobility. By the time he died, in 1543, Holbein had produced some of the finest portraits of his time.

DIEGO VELÁZQUEZ

PORTRAIT OF
JUAN DE PAREJA

Juan de Pareja was a slave who worked for Velázquez and became his assistant. Velázquez eventually granted Juan his freedom and he painted this portrait during their visit to Rome in 1650. The painting clearly shows Velázquez's ability to conjure up a character using only a very few colors and loose brushstrokes. He used long-handled brushes so that he could stand back from the canvas and see the effect as he worked.

For the tunic Velázquez used a technique known as "scumbling." This involves painting in two layers, putting on the second layer so that the lower coat is not completely covered. This uneven effect suggests the texture of the cloth and the play of light and shadow. Patches of thicker, grey paint pick out the highlights.

Velázquez exhibited this portrait during his visit to Rome and he became as popular in Italy as he was in his native Spain.

When viewed from a distance, Juan has a collar of fine white lace. When viewed close up, his collar becomes a series of loose, thick, white brushstrokes.

LAS MENINAS The Maids of Honour (detail)

This actual painting extends twice as high as the area shown here and stands over 10 feet high. It shows the Princess Margarita, two of her maids of honor, and several other members of the Spanish royal court. The artist himself appears, at work on a huge canvas, on the left. He is actually painting a portrait of the king and queen, whose blurred reflections can be seen in the mirror at the back of the room.

Velázquez is playing games with what the viewer might expect to see in a painting of the Spanish royal family—with the king and queen dominating the painting. In fact, nearly everyone in the painting is looking at the king and queen, but they themselves only appear in a mirror image.

POPE INNOCENT X

Velázquez painted the pope's face so accurately that the pope said the result was "too truthful." He probably did not like the ruthless expression that the artist had captured. In this portrait the different materials of the sitter's clothes are painted superbly, giving a sense of great richness and power.

Velázquez proudly included his own portrait in Las Meninas. *It shows him in 1656, aged 57.*

Diego Velázquez was born in 1599 in Seville, Spain. He was apprenticed to Seville's leading art teacher when he was 12 and started to produce paintings in his own name at the age of 18. From the beginning, he specialized in paintings of people. In 1623 he moved to Madrid, where he soon became the favorite painter of King Philip IV. He remained court painter until his death in 1660, and produced portraits of the king, queen, and the rest of the royal family. He also made two long visits to Italy, where he looked at the works of the great Italian artists, chose pictures to decorate the royal palace in Madrid, and painted the portrait of the pope.

REMBRANDT VAN RIJN

SELF-PORTRAIT

Rembrandt painted around one hundred self-portraits. This is one of his last, completed in 1669, a few months before he died at the age of 63.

Rembrandt's self-portraits act as a visual diary over forty years, showing his development from hopeful young artist, through his middle years as a successful painter, to his old age alone in his studio. They are often very moving in their honesty, showing a man who enjoyed life but who had suffered; only one of his children survived him. Rembrandt did not attempt to flatter himself: in this portrait he shows himself looking old, wrinkled, and sad.

Rembrandt was especially interested in the effects of light and shadow. He used shadow to provide depth and atmosphere, and light to pick out the most important areas in a picture and to model shapes. In this portrait everything is in shadow except the head, which has been lit up.

Rembrandt used tiny touches of paint to lighten parts of the face, such as the tip of his nose and his cheeks.

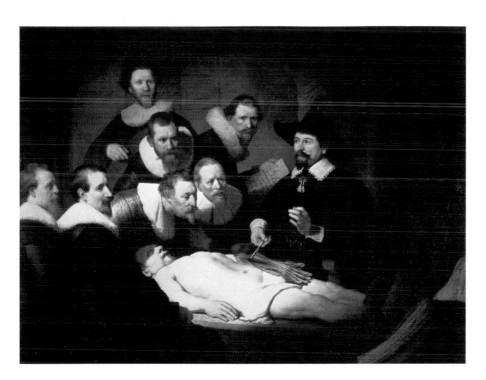

ANATOMY LESSON OF DR. TULP

It was fashionable in Rembrandt's time for guilds and societies to commission group portraits of their members. The people were usually arranged in neat rows, looking straight at the artist. When Dr. Nicholas Tulp, head of the Guild of Surgeons in Amsterdam, asked Rembrandt to paint a group portrait, Rembrandt took a new approach. The surgeons in *The Anatomy Lesson of Dr. Tulp* look as if they are fascinated by what is going on. They stare at the dissected corpse, which Rembrandt has lit brightly, making it, not the people, the center of attention.

PORTRAIT OF SASKIA

All through his life Rembrandt made prints and drawings. When he became engaged to Saskia van Uylenburch in 1633, he drew this gentle portrait of his bride-to-be. The careful drawing of her face contrasts with the rapid strokes he used for her clothes. Rembrandt was fascinated by Saskia's face and after their marriage she became his favorite model.

Rembrandt painted this self-portrait in 1629. He was 23 and still lived in his home town of Leiden.

Rembrandt van Rijn was born in 1606 in the town of Leiden in the Netherlands. He was apprenticed to a local artist but soon moved to the city of Amsterdam where there was more work. In Amsterdam he married Saskia.

Rembrandt became a popular artist, producing numerous paintings, drawings, and prints. Towards the end of his life, his art was less popular. He sold fewer paintings, but carried on spending a lot of money buying works of art. As a result he had large debts and had to sell his collection. Although it included many of his own works, the collection only fetched 600 guilders, less than Rembrandt had been paid for a single painting earlier in his career. He died a poor man in 1669.

JAN VERMEER

GIRL WITH A PEARL EARRING

This painting is unusual for Vermeer, with its dark, unrecognizable background and the girl's exotic headdress. There are no clues in the portrait as to the identity of the girl.

The smooth surface of her skin was painted by brushing on several layers of transparent flesh-color over a solid layer of under-painting. This technique, known as glazing, was ideal for giving a smooth, subtle finish.

Vermeer was well known for his treatment of light. In this portrait he brightens up the face by including tiny highlights. The highlights in the eyes seem to give added life to the girl's expression. When the painting was restored in 1994, two further, even smaller, highlights were discovered at either end of the mouth. Although the portrait was carefully posed, it seems as if the artist has caught the girl's quick glance, as her eyes meet our own.

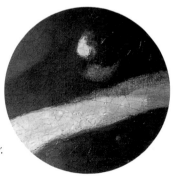

The bright highlights on the pearl earring were painted using only two brushstrokes of white paint, showing the bright reflection of the light coming from the left, and the paler reflection from her collar.

THE LACEMAKER

Vermeer's lacemaker concentrates closely on her work in this tiny painting (only 9.3 by 8 inches). The artist focuses on the lacemaking by placing highlights on her fingers and her face. The Dutch middle classes, who bought Vermeer's paintings, valued hard work as a virtue and would have recognized the lacemaker as a good and hard-working woman.

Vermeer painted this view of his home town, Delft, in 1660–61.

THE MUSIC LESSON

Many of Vermeer's settings are typical of Dutch seventeenth century houses. The rooms have white walls, black-and-white tiled floors, and windows with tiny panes of glass. The artist always arranged the objects in the room carefully to get the right effect. In *The Music Lesson* the chair, viol, and wine jug probably belonged to the artist; the painting on the wall belonged to his mother in law; and the virginal (an early keyboard instrument) was probably borrowed especially for the painting. The woman's face can only be seen reflected in the mirror, and part of Vermeer's easel can also be made out in the reflection.

Jan Vermeer was born in the Dutch port of Delft in 1632. He lived and worked in the town and was taught by a local artist. Most of his pictures are of people, many in middle-class Dutch houses. They are known for their fine handling of color and composition.

Little is known for certain about Vermeer's life and there is no surviving portrait or self-portrait of the artist. Vermeer did not produce many paintings and fewer than forty of his works survive. For years after his death in 1675, Vermeer's artistic work was largely ignored by collectors and artists. Then in 1866, a French writer, W. Thoré-Bürger, rediscovered his work. Since then, Vermeer's paintings have been recognized as the masterpieces they are.

PIERRE-AUGUSTE RENOIR

GIRL WITH A FAN

The actress Jeanne Samary was a friend of Renoir's and he painted her portrait several times. In 1881, when he painted this portrait of the actress, there was a craze in Europe for Japanese arts and crafts. Jeanne is holding a Japanese fan in the painting.

The portrait shows how Renoir could change his technique to suit whatever he was painting. The colorful flowers in the background and on Jeanne's hat are painted in a typical Impressionist style, with loose dots and "curls" of paint, to give the impression of the petals. The design on the fan is portrayed with a few colored squiggles that conjure up a figure and some swirling Japanese writing. But Jeanne's face is painted using a different technique, with more feathery strokes blending together to suggest the softness of her skin.

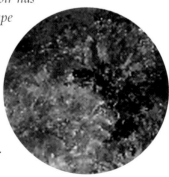

Renoir has built up the shape and color of the flowers with loose brushstrokes of white and pink, finally adding brilliant highlights of bright red.

THE LOGE

This is a portrait of Renoir's young brother Edmond and a model called Nini. They are in a "loge" ("box") at the theater. Renoir seems to have been more interested in Nini than Edmond, who hovers in the background with his opera glasses. Nini is painted with much greater care. Renoir used thin layers of paint on her face and neck, and small touches of thicker paint to highlight her pearls and the lace at her neckline.

THE BOATING PARTY

This group portrait shows some friends enjoying themselves at a riverside restaurant one Sunday afternoon. Several of the people in the picture are known to be friends of the artist. The woman with the dog is the model Aline Charigot, whom Renoir was soon to marry.

This self-portrait was painted in 1910 when Renoir was an old man.

Pierre-Auguste Renoir was born in Limoges, France, in 1841. When he was 13 he got his first job, painting flowers on dishes in a porcelain factory. In 1862 he began to study art, and went to Paris where he met painters Claude Monet and Alfred Sisley. The three artists began to take their easels outdoors and to paint in the open air in the loose, colorful Impressionist style.

Renoir's main interest was in painting people. As well as individual portraits he produced paintings of groups of people in the streets, family groups, and people enjoying themselves outdoors. He especially liked painting women and children, and he captured their fresh prettiness in a soft, delicate style. By the time he died in 1919 he had produced more than 6,000 paintings.

VINCENT VAN GOGH

SELF-PORTRAIT

This was the last of Van Gogh's self-portraits, painted in 1889, the year before he died. The stern expression and lined face belong to a man who has had a troubled life. In this self-portrait Van Gogh has handled the paint with great skill and produced an artistic style of tremendous power.

All the brushstrokes can be seen clearly. As they swirl this way and that, they follow the curves of Van Gogh's hair, the lines on his face, the textures of his jacket. In the background are more swirls. Van Gogh has highlighted his left eye with a lighter color which has made his stare appear strong and penetrating. The reddish colors of his beard and hair are the only warm colors in the painting. When the picture was finished, Van Gogh gave it to his friend and doctor, Paul Gachet. It must have been a vivid reminder of the doctor's patient.

Van Gogh laid on the paint thickly, using a large brush or a palette knife to apply the blues and greens. In some places the paint stands up above the surface of the canvas in ridges.

34

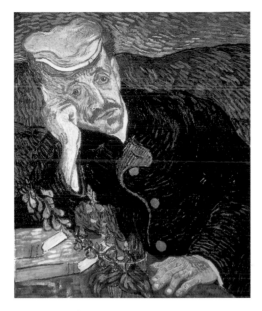

Portrait of Dr. Gachet
This portrait is painted with strong dashes of paint, in different colors, which merge together when viewed from a distance. The deep blues contrast with the color of the doctor's face.

THE YELLOW CHAIR

Van Gogh's painting of his chair is a kind of self-portrait without the sitter. Van Gogh saw it as an image of his loneliness—the chair stands on its own, outlined with dark paint and untouched by any other furniture in the room. A simple peasant's chair on a rough tiled floor, it also suggests that Van Gogh was closer to country people than to the artists and cafés of Paris.

The Price of Art

Van Gogh painted hundreds of portraits. He often completed a painting in a single day—a remarkable speed for any artist. But Van Gogh sold very few paintings in his own lifetime. He wrote, "I cannot help it, that my paintings do not sell. The time will come when people will see that they are worth more than the price of the paint." In May 1990, 100 years after his death, Van Gogh's *Portrait of Dr. Gachet* sold for US $82,500,000—the highest price ever paid for a painting at an auction.

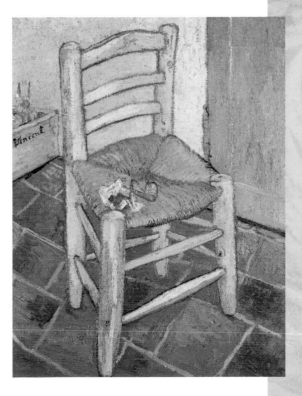

Van Gogh painted this self-portrait at the beginning of 1889, just after he had cut off his left earlobe.

Born in 1853, Vincent Van Gogh was the son of a Dutch clergyman. As a young man he had a series of different jobs, including those of teacher and trainee priest. Van Gogh taught himself to draw and paint and developed his own unique style. His paintings were so unusual that few people bought, or even knew about, his work.

Van Gogh lived in Paris for several years and then rented a house in the South of France. He invited his friend and fellow artist, Gauguin, to stay but in 1888 they had a huge argument and Van Gogh flew at Gauguin with a knife. That evening Van Gogh cut off part of his own left ear. After some time in hospital he seemed to get better, but in 1890 Van Gogh shot himself in the chest and died two days later.

PABLO PICASSO

WEEPING WOMAN

In the late 1930s Picasso painted several pictures in response to the suffering caused by the civil war in Spain. One of these was *Weeping Woman*, a portrait of Picasso's friend, Dora Maar.

This picture is a powerful expression of grief and anguish. The woman holds a white handkerchief to her face, but Picasso has painted it as if it were transparent, so we can see her mouth through the fabric. The fingers that hold the handkerchief to her face seem to turn into the tears that stream from her eyes. Picasso has used bright stylized colors which are not naturalistic. These clashing colors, the lines on her face, the way she is biting the material of the handkerchief between her teeth, all express her sorrow and create a feeling of unbearable suffering.

A large, oval tear, which could also be the nail of a finger holding the handkerchief, drips down the woman's cheek.

OLD JEWISH MAN WITH A BOY

During his "blue period," Picasso painted poor people on the streets of Barcelona. Their sad expressions, bony feet and begging posture show their poverty—and Picasso's sympathy for them.
No one knows for certain why Picasso painted them in blue, although the strange color combines with the bare settings to give the painting a cold, sad atmosphere.

This photograph of Picasso was taken in 1953, when he was 72.

Pablo Picasso was born in Malaga, Spain, in 1881. He was the son of a professor of art who recognized his son's talent at a very early age. After training at the Academy of Fine Arts in Barcelona, Picasso moved to Paris, where he lived for much of his life.

In the early twentieth century, Paris was the home of many artists and saw the birth of many new artistic styles. Picasso's own style changed dramatically as the years went by. He explored each new style he had found with huge energy and excitement, but then moved on with equal excitement to a completely different approach.

More than 20,000 paintings, drawings, sculptures, prints, and other works poured from his studio until his death in 1973, making him the most famous and most important of twentieth century artists.

PORTRAIT OF DANIEL-HENRY KAHNWEILER

Daniel-Henry Kahnweiler was a writer and art dealer who helped Picasso as a young artist. As he was one of the first to recognize the quality of Picasso's cubist work, it was appropriate that Picasso should paint a cubist portrait of him. Cubism is a style that breaks up the subject into angular shapes but keeps some recognizable features so that viewers can put the subject back together again in their imagination. In this painting the sitter's long nose, eyes, gloved hands, coat button, and watch chain can be seen.

FRIDA KAHLO

THE FRAME

The Mexican artist Frida Kahlo painted many self-portraits. Some describe the suffering and pain she endured as the result of a horrific accident she had as a young girl, others show her with flowers or even butterflies in her hair, and with the parrots and monkeys that she kept as pets.

In this self-portrait Kahlo is surrounded by a decorative frame of flowers and birds. The decoration is painted in the style of a traditional Mexican mirror, giving the impression that Frida is looking at her own reflection. The painting of her head, which is done in oils on metal, is highly detailed, with thin delicate brushstrokes. Frida Kahlo studied her own face carefully as she painted. She worked methodically from the top of the head to the bottom. The decorative "frame," by contrast, is painted in loose splashes of color that catch the eye but direct the viewer's gaze to the portrait.

The decoration of the birds and flowers is painted on the back of the glass that covers the portrait itself, so that it overlaps the actual painting of Frida.

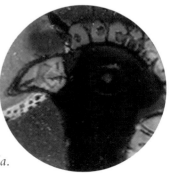

FRIDA AND DIEGO RIVERA

Frida Kahlo painted herself with her husband, the artist Diego Rivera. The plain background and stiff poses of this painting are taken from the style of popular, naive Mexican painting, which both the artists liked. Kahlo placed the couple's clasped hands exactly at the center of the canvas, to show how important the marriage was to her. The dove above her head carries a banner which records the date of the picture, the names of Frida and Diego, and the fact that the artist painted it in San Francisco, California.

Frida Kahlo in 1951, aged 44.

Frida Kahlo was born in Mexico in 1907. Her father was a Hungarian who had emigrated to Mexico and her mother was a Mexican. She learned to paint from her father, who was a photographer and amateur painter. She was fascinated by his portrait photographs and the poses of many of her portraits are similar to those her father used in his studio photographs.

Frida Kahlo married Mexico's most famous artist, mural painter Diego Rivera, in 1929. They had a stormy marriage with very happy times and huge arguments. For much of the time they lived in separate houses, built next to one another and connected by a bridge, so that they could escape into privacy when they wanted to. After a series of illnesses, Frida Kahlo died in 1954.

A Long Illness

This photograph shows Frida Kahlo in her studio with her doctor. She is holding a palette of oil paints. Her painting of herself and the doctor is still hanging on the easel. For much of her life Frida was unwell. She had polio as a child, was severely injured in a traffic accident as a teenager and had endless operations as an adult. Frida Kahlo's doctor helped Frida through her illnesses and became a good friend.

PROPORTIONS

The mathematical relationships between different parts of the face and how they combine to make up the whole are known as the proportions. Portrait painters need to know how human proportions work so that they can work out, for instance, the size of a nose in relation to a mouth and where it should best be placed. This helps artists paint both "ideal" (the most perfect) beauty and the different faces of ordinary people. It is often the variations from the "ideal" that are the most interesting. The artist can also play all sorts of tricks on the viewer by distorting the proportions.

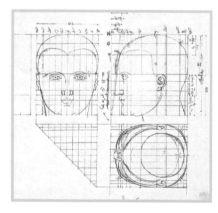

DÜRER'S STUDIES AND PAINTINGS

Albrecht Dürer (1471–1528) wrote a book about the proportions of the human body. He worked out the "ideal" proportions of the human head and wrote about the differences in people's appearances and how these actual differences make faces interesting. In the drawings on the left Dürer has studied the head from different angles. *Four Apostles* shows how Dürer used these studies in his paintings. When a head looks down, for instance, the area of the forehead appears much larger and the lower part of the face is squashed.

Four Apostles
(detail)
Albrecht Dürer

40

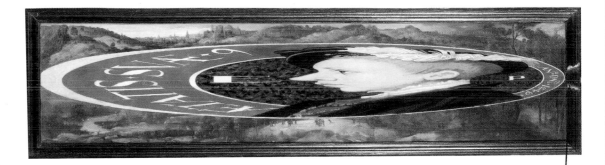

viewing notch

PORTRAIT OF PRINCE
EDWARD VI *William Scrots, died 1554*

Viewed from the front in the usual way, this portrait of Edward VI (above) is very distorted. The pointed nose and squashed head look like a grotesque caricature. Only the background landscape is in the right proportions. This kind of painting is called an "anamorphosis." If you look at the picture close up from the right hand side, from the special viewing notch provided in the frame, a true-to-life portrait of the boy can be seen. Even the inscription of Edward's initials E P can be read easily. This clever portrait was probably painted as a present to amuse the young prince.

The view, at an angle, from the viewing notch at the right hand side

CEILING FROM THE PAINTED ROOM,
DUCAL PALACE, MANTUA *Andrea Mantegna, 1431–1506*

In this painted ceiling, Italian artist Mantegna creates the illusion that we are looking up at a real scene. The ceiling of the room seems to have a circular hole, open to the sky. Mantegna has used all his skill to play this trick. The heads of the infants who look down on the room below are squashed and shortened, so that it looks as if we are viewing normal faces from a long way below. The ladies of the court and the servants look as if they are peering down at us, over the edge.

CARICATURE

A caricature is a portrait in which some of the features are exaggerated or distorted to produce a comic effect. The idea is to reveal the person's character through their physical features. Leonardo da Vinci's grotesque heads show his fascination with the way people's characters show in their faces. Artists were quick to realize that people could, for example, be drawn as if they were grossly fat, to show greed; or someone very vain could be drawn with a huge head.

Caricature soon became a way of criticizing people and of attacking enemies—especially political enemies. The work of the great eighteenth and nineteenth century caricaturists was published in newspapers and magazines, giving amusement to thousands of people every week.

LES POIRES,

PEARS (King Louis Philippe)
Charles Philipon, 1806–1862
A French newspaper cartoonist drew King Louis of France as a pear. Readers instantly recognized the image. The French word for "pear" ("poire") also means "idiot," so it is not surprising that the king was offended and the paper's editor was fined for the insult. The editor then published this group of drawings as a reply, to show how similar to a pear the king's face actually was!

GROTESQUE HEADS
Leonardo da Vinci, 1452–1519
Leonardo was fascinated by ugly or unusual-looking people and would follow them through the streets, memorizing their features.

A Grotesque Old Woman *16th century (Possibly painted by the Flemish artist, Quentin Massys)*

The Ugly Duchess *John Tenniel, 1820 1914 Tenniel's original illustration for* Alice's Adventures in Wonderland.

A MODEL FOR THE UGLY DUCHESS

The grotesque head (above left) was painted in the early sixteenth century. The old woman is wearing a low-cut dress and fashionable head-dress that would look better on a younger woman. The artist is making the point that old people should not try to pretend to be younger than they actually are. Many experts think that the painting is meant to show Margaretha Maultasch, Duchess of Carinthia and Tyrol, who was famed at the time as the ugliest woman in the world! This painting was later used as a model for one of the characters in Lewis Carroll's book, *Alice in Wonderland*. The illustration of the Ugly Duchess (above right) shows that the artist, John Tenniel, based the image of the duchess on the Grotesque Old Woman. Tenniel used the old portrait but created a new and unique character for the Alice books.

FACES AROUND THE WORLD

Faces have been depicted in a huge variety of artistic styles by different peoples throughout the world. Paintings and sculptures have been made of many of the world's powerful rulers, but artists have also captured the faces of more ordinary people in many different situations. Images of faces are also important in many of the world's religions. These paintings and sculptures provide a fascinating visual record of different civilizations and their artistic traditions.

HEAD OF THE BUDDHA *5th century*
This religious sculpture was made in north-west India. It has the signs of the sacred figure of the Buddha: a hair knot, forehead mark and elongated earlobes which show that he used to be a prince and wear long, heavy earrings. This graceful head would originally have been painted with naturalistic colors.

HEAD OF A KING *12th–15th century*
This elegant bronze head was made by the Yoruba people of Nigeria, Africa, in a naturalistic style. It was probably decorated with real beads and the holes were made for a moustache of real hair.

A KUBA KING *1750–1800*
Statues like this one were made to
commemorate the kings of the Kuba people
of Zaire, in Africa. The different rulers were
depicted by almost identical statues, with a
few clues as to the identity of the king, such
as the game board which is on the base of
this statue. These statues were symbols of
royal power, built to show how strong the
kings were at this time.

EMPEROR SHAH JAHAN *Bichitr, 1630*
This portrait of the Indian Emperor who built the Taj Mahal was
painted during the Mughal period when naturalistic portraiture
became popular in Indian art. The Emperor Shah Jahan admired
English miniatures (see page 25) and this painting uses a mixture
of European and Indian artistic styles. The Emperor is shown in
traditional clothes and jewelery and the halo around his head
emphasizes his royal power. Shah Jahan described the painting as
"a good portrait of me in my fortieth year."

LU MING AND HIS WIFE *1740–1780*

"Ancestor portraits" like these were found in the homes of many Chinese people. They were only brought out on special occasions and were displayed when prayers were offered to the spirits of dead members of the family. This pair shows Lu Ming, an important official, together with his wife. Their portraits were painted onto two silk panels. The artist has used bright colors to show the detail of their highly decorated clothes, embroidered with flowers and dragons, which contrast with the calm, still expressions of the faces.

PERUVIAN HEAD *6th–9th century*

This pottery head was made by the Moche people who lived on the northern desert coast of Peru. Many heads in this style have been found and the features on each of the faces are different, suggesting that they were modeled to look like individual people. No one knows why they have the large, curved ring on top of the heads. This particular head shows the markings of a Moche ruler .

A PICNIC SCENE *c.1600*

Tiles like these would have decorated one of the royal pavilions in Persia (now called Iran) where picnics like this would have taken place. This scene has been painted using brilliant colors. The patterns on the clothes and the trees and flowers create a very decorative effect. The elegant figures have been drawn with clear, flowing lines and gently tilted heads, giving them a graceful, dance-like appearance.

The features of the faces have been painted with simple, black lines. This young man is wearing an elaborate turban.

NAKAMURA SHIKAN
Kunichica, 1835–1900

This is a Japanese print of the actor Nakamura Shikan. It is a traditional stylized "actor portrait" with an exaggerated expression. In this picture the black dots of the upturned pupils of his eyes, the "V" shape of his eyebrows and the turned-down corners of his mouth give him an angry glare.

INDEX